Cocker Spaniels

ABDO
Publishing Company

A Buddy Book
by
Julie Murray

VISIT US AT
www.abdopub.com

Published by Buddy Books, an imprint of ABDO Publishing Company, 4940 Viking Drive, Suite 622, Edina, Minnesota 55435. Copyright © 2005 by Abdo Consulting Group, Inc. International copyrights reserved in all countries. No part of this book may be reproduced in any form without written permission from the publisher.

Printed in the United States.

Edited by: Christy DeVillier
Contributing Editors: Matt Ray, Michael P. Goecke
Graphic Design: Maria Hosley
Image Research: Deborah Coldiron
Photographs: American Kennel club, Corel, Fotosearch, PhotoSpin

Library of Congress Cataloging-in-Publication Data

Murray, Julie, 1969-
   Cocker spaniels/Julie Murray.
      p. cm. — (Animal kingdom. Set II)
   Includes bibliographical references and index.
   Contents: The dog family — Cocker spaniels — What they're like — Coat and color — Size — Care — Feeding — Things they need — Puppies.
   ISBN 1-59197-307-4
      1. Cocker spaniels—Juvenile literature. [1. Cocker spaniels. 2. Spaniels. 3. Dogs.] I. Title.

SF429.C55M87 2003
636.752'4—dc21

                                        2002043623

Contents

The Dog Family

What do dogs and wolves have in common? They both belong to the Canidae family. Dogs are related to foxes, dingoes, and jackals, too.

At one time, dogs were wild like wolves. Nobody is sure when dogs became tame. Today, millions of people have pet dogs.

Foxes are related to dogs.

Some dogs belong to one breed. The American Kennel Club has named about 150 dog breeds. A few of them are dalmatians, beagles, and cocker spaniels.

Dalmatian

Beagle

Cocker spaniel

Cocker Spaniels

Spaniels have been around for hundreds of years. The first spaniels may have lived in Spain. Today, there are different breeds of spaniels. Cocker spaniels are the smallest spaniels.

Cocker spaniels lived in England long ago. They were trained to help people hunt birds. They often hunted woodcocks. This is how the cocker spaniel got its name.

Today, there are two breeds of cocker spaniels. They are American and English. They belong to the sporting dogs group. Golden retrievers and Irish setters are sporting dogs, too.

A woodcock

American
cocker spaniel

English
cocker spaniel

Cocker Spaniel Breeds

American
cocker spaniel

English
cocker spaniel

What They Look Like

American cocker spaniels grow to become about 14 inches (36 cm) tall at their shoulders. Adults may weigh between 24 and 32 pounds (11 and 15 kg). English cocker spaniels grow a bit bigger.

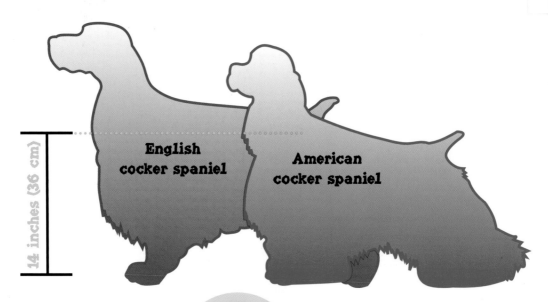

14 inches (36 cm)

English cocker spaniel

American cocker spaniel

Cocker spaniels have long ears and shiny coats. Some have hair that lies flat. Others have wavy hair.

This cocker spaniel has wavy hair.

Some cocker spaniels are one solid color. They are commonly black, brown, autumn-red, tan, or cream. Parti-colored cocker spaniels have two or more colors. They may be black and white, tan and white, or black and tan.

A parti-colored cocker spaniel

Cocker Spaniels As Pets

Cocker spaniels are great pets. People love them for many reasons. Cocker spaniels are loving, cheerful, and gentle. These playful dogs enjoy being part of the family. They get along well with children and other family pets.

Grooming And Care

    Grooming is important for all dogs. Brushing a dog's coat keeps it smooth and clean. Owners should brush their cocker spaniels four times a week.

    Dogs need their nails clipped short. Cleaning a dog's teeth and ears is also important. Ask a **veterinarian** how to do this.

Pet stores sell special brushes for grooming dogs.

A **veterinarian** is a doctor for animals. Taking pets to a veterinarian helps them stay healthy.

Feeding And Exercise

All dogs need food and fresh water every day. Adult cocker spaniels should be fed once a day. Do not change a dog's food too often. A changing diet can lead to health problems.

Dogs need exercise. Some people take their dogs for walks. Some people play with their dogs in a fenced yard. Exercise helps cocker spaniels stay healthy and happy.

Exercise is good for cocker spaniels.

Tags

It is important for dogs to wear a collar with tags. These tags should have the owner's name, address, and phone number. This helps people find a lost dog's home.

Owner's Name
Address
Phone Number

Puppies

Cocker spaniels commonly have litters of four to six puppies. The puppies are born blind and deaf. They drink their mother's milk. Puppies will begin seeing and hearing at about two weeks old.

A cocker spaniel puppy

Puppies should stay with their mother for eight weeks. Cocker spaniels may live as long as 14 years.

Becoming the owner of a puppy is exciting. Caring for a puppy also means training it. Some people train their dogs with help from puppy schools. There, puppies learn to obey their owners. They learn commands such as "sit" and "stay."

Some cocker spaniels
learn to be show dogs.

Learning to be friendly with other
dogs is an important lesson. At puppy
schools, puppies can play with other
dogs. They meet new people there, too.

Important Words

breed a special group of dogs. Dogs of the same breed look alike.

diet the food that a dog (or a person) normally eats.

groom to clean and care for.

litter the group of puppies born at one time.

veterinarian a doctor for animals. A short name for veterinarian is "vet."

Web Sites

To learn more about cocker spaniels, visit ABDO Publishing Company on the World Wide Web. Web sites about cocker spaniels are featured on our Book Links page. These links are routinely monitored and updated to provide the most current information available.

www.abdopub.com

Index